"I took my youth group through this material; it was easy for me to use as a leader. The questions were right on target to the students' needs, and their response to the material was excellent.

"I believe this series will be very beneficial in challenging students to be more like Christ."

> Rick Wilson
> Minister to Youth
> Fort Valley, Georgia

"Bill Jones has that unique ability as a communicator (whether speaking or writing) to 'scratch where people itch.' Teenagers trust him. Adults respect him. Although immensely gifted, his appeal is a result of his spiritual integrity. Bill 'walks the talk.'"

> Tommy Gilmore
> Director of Student Ministries
> Roanoke, Virginia

"God used these studies in my church in a mighty way. There has never been a generation for which this series is more relevant. Every youth should read them."

> Dana Mathewson
> Minister of Youth
> Pasadena, Texas

"These Bible studies provide an open forum for young people. They'll find practical applications for Scriptural principles."

> Keith Geren
> Youth Pastor
> Miami, Florida

Other Here's Life books—

Parents:

Raising Them Properly

Bill Jones

Here's Life Publishers

First printing, July 1988

Published by
HERE'S LIFE PUBLISHERS, INC.
P. O. Box 1576
San Bernardino, CA 92402

ISBN 0-89840-208-5
LOC Catalog Card Number 88-80445

For More Information, Write:
Student Mission Impact – P. O. Box 2200, Stone Mountain, GA 30086
L.I.F.E. – P.O. Box A399, Sydney South 2000, Australia
Campus Crusade for Christ of Canada – Box 300, Vancouver, B.C., V6C 2X3, Canada
Campus Crusade for Christ – Pearl Assurance House, 4 Temple Row, Birmingham, B2 5HG, England
Lay Institute for Evangelism – P.O. Box 8786, Auckland 3, New Zealand
Campus Crusade for Christ – P.O. Box 240, Colombo Court Post Office, Singapore 9117
Great Commission Movement of Nigeria – P.O. Box 500, Jos, Plateau State Nigeria, West Africa
Campus Crusade for Christ International – Arrowhead Springs, San Bernardino, CA 92414, U.S.A.

Dedicated to Jeff and Gina Paglialonga,
former students in our youth ministry,
who honored the Lord as they obeyed their parents
(Colossians 3:20)

A Special Thanks

To Chris Frear for his editing and encouragement.

To Velva Tignor and Kari Knowles for typing the manuscript.

To the Here's Life staff for their enthusiasm, support and help.

To the youth ministries across the country who field-tested this material.

Contents

Foreword

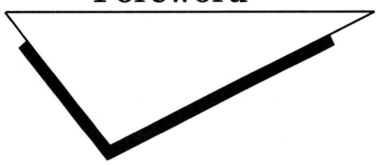

It's tough being a teenager—especially at home. Parents are trying to keep things under control and kids are trying to get on with their lives. In the process, you sometimes may feel misunderstood, held back, mistrusted, maybe even unloved.

I can't think of a better person than Bill Jones to help you work through how to improve things at home. Bill has worked with young people all his life. He speaks to thousands of students every year. He knows the problems from your perspective. Yet he has worked with many parents as well—in fact, he has four kids of his own! He knows from experience how parents think.

More than that, Bill is well acquainted with what the Bible says, and he will help you understand how it applies to parents. Did you ever think about the fact that Jesus had to relate to parents, too? And sometimes *He* had problems communicating with them. Find out how He handled things, what He said, and what He did.

I'll be surprised if you don't think that this study was made just for you. It's that down-to-earth in the things kids are dealing with every day. And it's not a lot of high-sounding advice. It is full of examples, questions, and items for discussion, all designed to help you decide what's important. It will help you think realistically about what can realistically be done to make your life the best it can be — for yourself, your parents, and the Lord.

Paul Fleischmann
Executive Director
National Network of Youth Ministries

Something to Think About . . .

Parents. What would you do without them? What can you do with them?

Parents are only as good as you train them to be. Yes—you have to *train* your parents if they're ever going to turn out the way you want them to.

It's your job to assume the responsibility for raising your parents properly. It's not an easy task either. It requires a lot from you.

First, raising parents takes patience. Since your parents probably won't change overnight, you'll need patience to keep from getting frustrated and giving up hope.

Second, it's going to take change on your part. You cannot simply *wish* your parents were different and then suddenly they become perfect.

If you want your parents to change, you need to help them. And for them to change, you must change. That's what this book is about—helping you change in order to help your parents become the very best.

Δ   Δ   Δ

Every year his parents went to Jerusalem for the Feast of the Passover. When he was twelve years old, they went up to the Feast, according to the custom. After the Feast was over, while his parents were returning home, the boy Jesus stayed behind in Jerusalem, but they were unaware of it. Thinking he was in their company, they traveled on for a day.

Then they began looking for him among their relatives and friends. When they did not find him they went back to Jerusalem to look for him. After three days they found him in the temple courts, sitting among the teachers, listening to them and asking them questions. Everyone who heard him was amazed at his understanding and his answers. When his parents saw him, they were astonished. His mother said to him, "Son, why have you treated us like this? Your father and I have been anxiously searching for you."

"Why were you searching for me?" he asked. "Didn't you know I had to be in my Father's house?" But they did not understand what he was saying to them.

Then he went down to Nazareth with them and was obedient to them. But his mother treasured all these things in her heart. And Jesus grew in wisdom and stature, and in favor with God and men.

Luke 2:41-52

Δ   Δ   Δ

My Parents Don't Understand Me!

Listen in on two typical conversations between students and their parents. Watch for ways in which the students have failed to train their parents.

Son: (Walks in door after school) Hey, Mom and Dad! I've decided what I want to study in college after I graduate.

Mom: What's that, honey?

Son: I want to be a high school football coach, so I'm going to be a phys. ed. major.

Dad: A what?!

Son: A phys. ed. major.

Mom: Wouldn't that be boring? You don't want to spend the rest of your life in a locker room do you? All those sweaty clothes and dirty towels and the aroma! It's enough to. . .

Son: Aw, Mom.

Dad: Son, don't you realize what it takes to get ahead in life? You need to become an engineer or a doctor or a lawyer. You can't earn a living as a coach. Very few become major college or pro coaches—and do you know how secure their jobs are? They might as well have a revolving door on the office.

Son: But Dad . . .

Mom: We want you to have the best things in life. You don't realize how much money it costs just to live decently. As a coach you could never . . .

Son: But I . . .

Dad: You just need to forget all about being a football coach. Come back later when you've thought it over some more.

Son: (Head down, slowly walking out of the room) Sure, Dad. Whatever you say.

Δ Δ Δ

Mom: Has anyone asked you to homecoming yet?

Daughter: No, not really.

Mom: What do you mean "not really"?

Daughter: Well, a couple of guys have asked, but I was hoping Jonathan would.

Mom: Do you still like him? I don't understand you! He doesn't give you the time of day. You could be going out with any guy you wanted, but you're waiting around for him. Is that why you have been sitting home for the last few weekends? You are *foolish* to continue liking him. How could any girl want to go out with him?

Daughter: But he's so . . .

Mom: You're so hard to figure out sometimes. You'll be miserable the rest of your life waiting for him. Get your head on straight, girl.

Daughter: But you don't understand . . .

Mom: What about Rick? Yeah, Rick. He's such a nice boy.

Daughter: Mommmm . . .

Mom: You know his father is very influential in town. He's sharp and his parent's are good friends of ours.

Daughter: (Walking away, in frustration) Thanks, Mom. I've got to be going. I'll see you later. (Quietly sighs) Oh, brother!

Δ Δ Δ

Think about the last time you and your parents had a conversation like the ones above. Describe what happened:

_____

_____

How did you feel?

_____

_____

How did you respond? (Notice how both the guy and the girl in the opening scenes stopped talking rather than trying to work through the disagreement.)

_____

_____

How often do you feel like your parents understand you?

☐ Never   ☐ More often than not
☐ Very seldom   ☐ Most of the time
☐ Some of the time   ☐ Always
☐ Half of the time

You might feel like you're the only one with this kind of problem, but there were times when even Jesus' parents didn't understand Him. Read Luke 2:41-51. Pay special attention to verses 48-50.

What happens to Jesus in these verses?

_____

_____

What was the reaction of Jesus' parents in verse 48?

☐ They were calm and in control.
☐ They were a bit concerned.
☐ They were anxious and astonished.

God understands teenagers and the struggles of growing up (after all, Jesus was once a squeaky-voiced teenager, too). Whenever you have hassles with life, you can always find the solutions in the Bible because God understands.

You may be thinking, "If Jesus was perfect, and His parents didn't understand Him, then I don't stand a chance!"

The truth is, you *do* have a chance . . . but you have to work at it. Here are some things you can do to help.

Find out why your parents don't always understand.

Why do your parents not understand you? (Think for a couple of minutes before answering this question.)

_____

_____

Did you think of these reasons?

1. They don't really know me.

2. They've forgotten what it was like to be a teenager.

3. They grew up in a different time.

Top Offenses in Public Schools

	1940	1982
1.	Talking	Rape
2.	Gum chewing	Robbery
3.	Making noise	Assault
4.	Running in the halls	Burglary
5.	Getting out of turn in line	Arson
6.	Wearing improper clothing	Bombings
7.	Not putting paper in trashcans	Murder
8.		Suicide

The three reasons listed may be problems, but they are also symptoms of an even bigger problem — lack of communication.

See the importance of effective communication.

Most of the problems your parents have in understanding you are solved if you communicate better. Remember, if you want your parents to change, you need to change. Communication is the first area to work on!

Many students, at the first hint that their parents don't understand, take the easy way out and just quit communicating. (Remember the son and the daughter in the opening scenes?) Sometimes this is done even when the parents *could* understand, given a little more time, information and patience. This lack of communication begins a destructive pattern: The less you communicate the less your parents understand so the less you communicate.

It won't take long before your parents don't understand anything about you, and you aren't communicating a thing to your parents. This creates an environment for conflict.

Has this ever happened between you and your parents? How often? Describe one incident.

_____

_____

_____

Now look back at verses 48 and 49 in Luke 2. What was the first thing Jesus did when His parents didn't understand why He had stayed in Jerusalem?

_____

_____

What kind of attitude do you think He had?

_____

_____

What has your attitude been? How does it differ from Jesus' attitude?

_____

_____

Avoid making excuses for not communicating.

For your parents to understand you, they need to know you. They'll never get to know you unless you communicate with them.

Communication is hard work! Like we talked about earlier, it's often easier to say nothing than to talk things out. Have you ever given any of these excuses to justify your lack of communication?

- We only end up fighting.
- They will make fun of me.
- They never listen to me anyway.

What other excuses have you used?

1. _____

2. _____

3. _____

Each of these excuses may seem legitimate, but the trouble with making excuses is that the problem is never taken care of. Excuses keep you from communicating; your parents will never have a chance to understand you.

Realize there will be times when your parents will not understand.

Regardless of how well or how often you communicate with your parents, there are times when they just will not understand.

Look again at verses 48 through 50 in Luke 2. In verse 48 Jesus' parents don't know what to think about Him. In verse 49 Jesus communicates—He tries to explain why He did what He did. Verse 50 says that His parents *still* didn't understand Him.

Read Psalm 27:9,10. What was the writer feeling?

_____

_____

You can always express your feelings to God when your parents don't understand.

It is important to note at this point that just because your parents don't *agree* with you doesn't mean that they don't *understand* you. They can understand and disagree at the same time. Even though you are raising them, they have lived much longer than you and you need to respect their ability to make wise decisions.

Eliminate any communication killers.

When your parents don't understand, it doesn't take long to form habits that kill communication. Some of these are:

The Silent Treatment. You don't speak at all to your parents (usually to "get even" for something).

The Last Word. This can be done with anger or with controlled politeness. You have to have the last word.

I'll Just Put Up With It. You say what you think your parents want to hear, then go out secretly and do what you want anyway.

Bigger, Better, Nicer. You tell your parents how much better your friends' parents are.

Running Away. You get so frustrated that you leave the room or the house to avoid further confrontation.

Dogging Them With Dogmatism. Your conversation is full of phrases such as "You *never*" or "*You always.*"

Bugging 'Em to Death. Here you believe that if you

pester them long enough you can get your way.

Shoot to Stun. You see no other way to win so you yell obscenities, stunning them and communicating that this is so serious you're totally out of character.

What are some other communication killers?

1._____

2._____

3._____

Which ones do you use most?

1._____

2._____

3._____

How will you eliminate these killers? Be specific. (You may need to read the point below for ideas.)

_____

_____

Learn better ways to communicate.

Different ways to communicate work best with different people. Below are some suggestions.

Every day tell both of your parents what went on during the day. Be specific. Explain not only what happened but also what you thought and how you felt about it. Ask for their opinion: "What do you think I should do?" When they answer, do it!

Spend at least one evening each week at home with your parents. Spend time with *them* – not the TV or the telephone.

When you disagree, look at the issues from their point of view. Explain how you see their position.

Pick appropriate times to ask for things. Make sure they are not busy. With real important issues, never ask them in the presence of friends or right before you need an answer (that puts them on the spot). Be prepared to give mature answers to any objections you anticipate.

Ask to establish a family council to meet once a month and discuss how the family is doing.

Put it in writing. Whenever you have a problem expressing something face to face with your parents, write them a note and leave it where they will see it but no one else will.

What are other ways you can improve your communication with your parents?

_____

_____

_____

Wrapping It Up

The key to getting your parents to understand you is to follow Jesus' example—*communicate.* In a phrase: *Open up!* Yes, it is hard, but the alternative is to live with parents who never understand you. What a drag that is.

If you want to raise your parents properly, begin working on your communication with them:

1. Determine why they don't understand you.
2. See the importance of communication.
3. Avoid excuses for not communicating.
4. Realize there will be times when they will never understand.
5. Eliminate communication killers.
6. Learn better ways to communicate.

Parents' Obedience School
Session #1

1. What is the main area of misunderstanding right now between you and your parents?

_____

_____

2. Why do you think your parents don't understand?

_____

_____

3. What effect will communication have on this problem?

_____

_____

4. If you tried communicating before, what happened?

_____

_____

5. What communication killers can you eliminate? How will you do it? (Be specific.)

_____

_____

6. What things will you do to communicate better?

_____

_____

Memorize Luke 2:50,51

My Parents Won't Let Me Do Anything!

Put on your helmet. Strap on your flak jacket. You're about to enter a combat zone. Watch how this conversation progresses from disagreement to armed hostility.

Daughter: I'm not really hungry. May I be excused?

Mother: Honey, are you sick? You didn't eat any breakfast.

Daughter: No, just really excited about the concert.

Mother: Dear, I already told you—we can't let you go tonight.

Daughter: What?!

Mother: I'm sorry, but Great Aunt Mary and Uncle Fred are going to be stopping by later today and spending tonight with us. They haven't seen you since you were two years old and they'd be disappointed if you weren't here.

Daughter: But this is the best group *ever!* They'll *never* come this close again!

Dad: Of course the group will come back. But your great aunt and uncle may not. After all, they're getting old. You need to be here tonight.

Daughter: But I promised I'd drive.

Dad: Oh? But you knew we were expecting you home.

Daughter: Aw, Dad. Can't I go? I mean, it's not just me.

It's Jenny and Melissa and Robin too!

Dad: They'll just have to make other arrangements.

Daughter: All my friends get to do what they want to do.

Dad: Case closed.

Δ   Δ   Δ

If that had been you, how would you've responded?

- Smile and say, "That's OK. I thought I would ask anyway."
- Begin to cry uncontrollably.
- Shout, "You make my life miserable. I never get to have any fun."
- Run to your room and slam the door.
- Beg, plead, whine and complain until you get your way.
- Tell your parents you don't care what they say. You are going to do it anyway.
- Remind them of all the times they let your older brothers and sisters do similar things.
- All of the above!

How did the daughter in the illustration above respond?

_____

_____

If you are like most students, you probably have been in a similar situation. Think about a recent head-on collision with your parents when they wouldn't let you do what you wanted to do.

Describe the situation:

_____

_____

_____

What was the outcome?

_____

_____

How did you feel?

_____

_____

How do you think your parents felt?

_____

_____

Like the girl above, many conflicts center around freedom — the ability to do what you want to do. Usually, there's not enough of it to please students, or it's not at the right times or in the right areas. How much freedom do you feel like your parents give you?

☐ None   ☐ Just right
☐ Not enough   ☐ Too Much

Give an example.

_____

_____

_____

Jesus also had parents who didn't let Him do things that He really wanted to do. Read Luke 2:41-51 again.
What was Jesus doing?

_____

_____

What did His parents want Him to do? What did Jesus end up doing?

_____

_____

What do you think Jesus was thinking? What verses give you the idea of His attitude?

_____

_____

The best example to follow is Christ's. This is true especially in your relationship with your parents.

In the story of Jesus in Luke 2, Jesus wanted to do one thing and His parents wanted Him to do another. Instead of confrontation, verse 51 says that He continued in subjection or submission.

When you want to do one thing and your parents want you to do another, do you always respond like Jesus did? (Not just in action, but in attitude.)

☐ Yes   ☐ No

Think back to your head-on collision with Mom and Dad. Whenever you do not respect or respond to your parents' authority you are being rebellious. Too strong a word? Not at all. Look up the definition of *rebel* in a dictionary.

Rebel: _____

_____

A rebellious heart says, "I'm going to do what I want to do, when I want to do it, how I want to do it, as long as I want to do it, with whomever I want to do it, and nobody is going to stop me." When authority (like a parent) is placed over an individual with this kind of attitude (like a kid), the result is *conflict*.

Different families fight in different ways. What are the fights like with your parents?

_____

_____

The student's weapons are limited, but each one is deadly. The longer a student has been fighting with his parents, the better trained he is in knowing how to use them. He knows when and how to use each weapon to inflict maximum pain.

You may recognize some of these weapons:

1. Complaining.
   - "All the other kids get to do it."
   - "I always have to stay home."

2. Criticism.
   - "You're behind the times!"
   - "You're not fair!"

3. Anger.
   - Slam doors.
   - Yell, shout, scream.

4. Silence
   - Sigh.
   - Roll eyes.

5. Running out.
   - Run to your room.
   - Run to a friend's.

Which weapons do you use?

_____

_____

A young person may win the fight with his parents by

strategically using these weapons. However, if he is a Christian, he will feel miserable about it afterward.

Think about how different Jesus' response was. We're going to look at some steps you can take to respond more like Jesus, but first you have to *desire* to respond lovingly toward your parents like Jesus. Pray Psalm 139:23,24 to God: "Search me, O God, and know my heart; test me and know my anxious thoughts. See if there is any offensive way in me, and lead me in the way everlasting."

If you desire to love your parents, read on. If not, talk this over with a more mature Christian and continue to pray about it.

See authority and rebellion from God's perspective.

Read 1 Samuel 15:22, 23. What does God think of rebellion?

Look back at this chapter's opening illustration. In what ways was the daughter rebellious?

Read Romans 13:1. How does this apply to your parents' authority over you?

Read Romans 13:2. How does this apply to your rebellion toward your parents?

Ask God and your parents for forgiveness.

Once you see your parents' authority and your rebel-lion from God's perspective, ask both God and your parents to forgive you for any rebellious attitudes you may have had.

Without the forgiveness of both God and your parents, walls build up. Ephesians 4:26,27 says, "In your anger do not sin: Do not let the sun go down while you are still angry, and do not give the devil a foothold." When is the deadline to ask your parents to forgive you? _____

Work on instant obedience.

Many times when you're asked to do something, you don't mind doing it — you just don't want to do it right then. But it's important to obey your parents like you obey the Lord — as quickly as possible.

In what ways have you put off obeying your parents?

_____

_____

Read Colossians 3:20. In what things are you to obey your parents?

_____

Even if your parents aren't Christians, why should you obey them? (Review Romans 13:1,2)

_____

_____

Is there ever a time when you should not obey them? (Read Acts 5:29).

_____

_____

The only time you should not obey your parents—in fact, cannot obey them—is when they require you to do anything that directly contradicts the Bible. (Ask your youth pastor to help you decide when this is the right thing to do.)

Work on your attitude.

Read Ephesians 6:1-3. What should your attitude be when you obey your parents?

_____

_____

What does it mean to honor your parents? What does the word *honor* imply?

_____

_____

What is the difference between "obeying" and "honoring" your parents? (*Hint:* One has to do with action and the other with attitude.)

_____

_____

Can you obey your parents without honoring them? Can you honor them without obeying them? How?

_____

_____

_____

Jesus' parents were poor and uneducated, yet He respected them. Why do *your* parents deserve respect?

_____

_____

Name two other ways to show them respect.

1. I will stop any griping and complaining.

2. _____

3. _____

Learn to look at things the way your parents look at them.

You'll understand your parents a lot better if you try to see things from their perspective. For practice, refer back to the opening scene. List three reasons the parents did not want their daughter to go to the concert.

1. _____

2. _____

3. _____

In your latest argument, why didn't your parents want you to do what you wanted?

_____

_____

Thank your parents for all they do for you.

To help develop feelings of gratitude toward your parents, regularly thank them for all they do for you. This will help you dwell on the positive instead of the negative.

List four things you are thankful for about your parents.

1. _____

2. _____

3. _____

4. _____

Learn to suggest creative alternatives.

When a difference comes up, don't demand your own way. Instead, tell your parents you want to obey them. Then suggest a creative alternative that would satisfy both of you. For practice, refer back to the opening illustration. Come up with three creative alternatives.

1. _____

2. _____

3. _____

When you and your parents can't agree, pray.

Often what you want is good and needed, even important. If your parents say "no" to these kinds of things, don't argue or whine. Pray.

Proverbs 21:1 says, "The king's heart is in the hand of the LORD; he directs it like a watercourse wherever he pleases." If God controls the hearts and minds of kings, then He controls the hearts and minds of your parents.

If you want something that you know is right but your parents don't agree with you, ask God to change their hearts. God will answer.

Check the possible ways God may answer you:

☐ Yes.   ☐ No.

☐ Yes, but not now.   ☐ Quit bugging me.

Remember, "yes" is not the only way God responds. God sometimes must answer "no" or "not now." Why? He wants to protect you from problems and provide you with the very best. If you are having a hard time understanding how that works, consider how you feel about going to the dentist. As a kid, you hated it because it hurt. If you asked your mom to leave you home she said no. But today you are better off for it—your teeth aren't falling out!

Wrapping It Up

One of the most common complaints kids have about their parents is "They won't let me do anything!" Jesus had the same problem at times. But instead of fighting to do what He wanted to do, He chose to honor and obey what His parents wanted Him to do.

To respond more like Jesus did, you must:

1. See authority and rebellion from God's perspective.
2. Ask forgiveness.
3. Work on instant obedience.
4. Work on a respectful attitude.
5. Look at things through the eyes of parents.
6. Express thanks.

When you are practicing these things, then your parents are more likely to listen when you give a creative alternative. If they don't accept any alternatives, you can still pray. But the main thing is to continue in subjection to them. In a phrase: *Bow down.* This sounds tough to do, but think about this: If you were a parent, what would you respond to? Why?

Remember, if you want your parents to change, work on yourself first.

Parents' Obedience School
Session #2

1. Make a list of things for which you need to ask God and your parents for forgiveness. After you have asked, write down their response.

_____

_____

2. During this week, tell your parents at least one thing

every day you are grateful for about them. At the end of the week, write down their response.

_____

_____

3. Ask your mom to name three ways you can better obey and honor your dad. List them here.

    1. _____

    2. _____

    3. _____

4. Ask your dad to name three ways you can better obey and honor your mom. List them here.

    1. _____

    2. _____

    3. _____

5. Put these six suggestions (from questions 3 and 4) in practice for a week. At the end of the week write down how you did and what happened.

_____

_____

_____

6. What difference did it make in your relationship with your parents?

_____

_____

Memorize Colossians 3:20

My Parents Don't Trust Me!

Trust is earned. Sometimes it's hard to earn, especially if you've slipped up in the past. Watch how the students in the scenes below miss the opportunity to earn their parents' trust and end up in a bad situation.

Daughter: (Walking in the front door, trying to be as quiet as possible.)

Dad: Do you know what time it is?

Daughter: (startled) Oh, Dad, I'm so sorry.

Dad: (sarcastically) "I'm *sooo* sorry." That's all we ever hear from you around here! Do you realize that you are 45 minutes late?!

Daughter: But I can explain! We went to get a Coke after the game and started talking. Before we realized it, we were late. I thought about calling but didn't want to wake you up.

Dad: (angrily) Excuses, excuses, excuses!! What were you and that good-for-nothing boy really doing that made you late?

Daughter: (upset) Nothing, Dad, honest!

Dad: I've talked to you over and over about being home on time. Go to your room. You can't be trusted with anything.

Daughter: (frustrated) But it was an oversight . . .

Δ Δ Δ

Son: (enthusiastically) Hey, Mom! Can I borrow the car? My new stereo came in today and I need to go pick it up.

Mom: Have you finished everything Dad wanted you to do?

Son: (easygoing) No, not yet. But I'll finish them when I get back.

Mom: (suspiciously) What all have you gotten done?

Son: (slowly, thinking of the best way to say it) Well . . . a little of everything. And it won't take me long to finish it all when I get back . . . Uh, where did you put the keys?

Mom: Why didn't you do it this morning?

Son: I wasn't feeling up to it, so I listened to a couple of new albums.

Mom: Why should I trust you to do your work this afternoon if you didn't do it this morning?

Δ Δ Δ

Mom: We won't be back until about 2 A.M. If you need anything, call the neighbors across the street.

Son: Have a good time. Is it OK if a couple of friends come over for a while?

Dad: Absolutely not! I don't want some wild party going on over here while we're gone.

Son: I wasn't planning on having a wild party. I was just going to have a couple of friends over!

Dad: Remember last year what happened?

Mom: It took me weeks to clean the carpet.

Son: I was different then.

Dad: Well, until we know we can trust you, you can't have anyone over. End of discussion.

Mom: (sweetly) Have a good time, darling.

Son: (dejected) Right!

Δ Δ Δ

One of the common complaints students have about their parents is "They don't trust me!"

What about you? Do your parents trust you?

Rate how much you think your parents trust you on the scale below.

1   2   3   4   5   6   7   8   9   10

They trust me
as far as they
can throw me.

They trust me
with their
bank accounts

This is a good reflection of how well you've been raising your parents. What have you done in the past week to make them trust you? For example, think of tasks or responsibilities they've given you and how you handled them.

1. _____

2. _____

3. _____

What have you done with those responsibilities to make them not trust you?

1. _____

2. _____

3. _____

In which of the following areas do your parents not trust you? Give an example for each one you check.

Area   **Example**

☐ Being out late   _____

☐ Use of the car   _____

☐ Who you have as friends   _____

☐ How you spend your money   _____

☐ What you do on dates   _____

☐ How you make decisions   _____

☐ Staying home alone   _____

☐ Places you go   _____

☐ Telling the truth   _____

☐ Buying your clothes   _____

☐ Doing your chores   _____

☐ Doing your school work   _____

Trust. With it, relationships are smooth. Without it, there is tension, suspicion and ultimately a lot of fights.

There are several reasons why parents may not trust their child, but one of the biggest is that their son or daughter has been *irresponsible* in the past.

What do the words *responsible* and *irresponsible* mean? (Look them up in a dictionary.)

_____

_____

Think about it — how much would you trust each of the following people? Rate them 1 to 10.

- Someone who always followed through on what he said he would do.____
- Someone who was responsible half of the time but apologized each time he didn't come through.____
- Someone who was never responsible but always had a good excuse.____
- Someone who was never responsible and never had a valid excuse.____

The same holds true with your parents! If you want to raise them so they trust you, you must be responsible. You must follow through on your commitments.

Let's see how this worked out in the life of Jesus. Go back to Luke 2 and answer these questions.

Read verse 43. What is the situation here?

_____

_____

Read verses 43 and 44. Why were Jesus' parents not worried?

_____

_____

Why do you think they assumed Jesus was with other travelers?

_____

_____

We're not told specifically, but from the surrounding verses and what we know about the rest of His life, it's fair to assume that Jesus was always responsible and His parents could trust Him. They could be confident He was doing what He should be doing.

If Jesus had been irresponsible before this, His parents (like any other parents) would have made sure their child was with them at the start of the journey.

Digging Deeper

You may wonder if Jesus was irresponsible for staying behind in Jerusalem. What you do think? Why?

_____

_____

Let's look at the choices: Either Jesus knew His parents were leaving or He didn't. Since Jesus was responsible, He would have left with the caravan when it left — had He known. Therefore, we can conclude that He didn't know they had gone. Joseph and Mary probably thought the others had told Jesus they were leaving. When Jesus did discover they were gone, He did the wisest thing and stayed out in the most obvious place for His parents to look for Him. (A good rule of thumb anytime you're separated from your parents.)

Conclusion: Jesus was responsible. It was His parents who didn't handle this situation well.

Notice, too, that afterward Jesus didn't blame His parents or hold it over their heads. Instead He obeyed them and loved them.

How much did Jesus' obedience mean to his parents? Read verse 51.

Jesus' parents could trust Him because He was responsible. The same can be true for you! The following are some practical steps to take to get your parents to trust you.

Realize that trust is built slowly but can be broken quickly.

Trust is like a savings account — you can make deposits and withdrawals. Every responsible action is a deposit. Every time you are irresponsible, you make a withdrawal. Withdrawals are so easy. If you aren't careful, you can bankrupt yourself.

Write out the last three deposits you made to the "trust account."

1. _____

2. _____

3. _____

How much did your actions add to your account?

_____

_____

Write down the last three withdrawals you made on the "trust account."

1. _____

2. _____

3. _____

How much did your actions deplete your account?

_____

_____

Where does your account stand now?

_____

_____

See responsibility from your parents' perspective.

Why do your parents want you to be responsible?

☐ Because they are basically evil people and they want me to suffer.

☐ Because they have a weird sense of humor and they think it's fun when I'm miserable.

☐ Because they love me and they are trying to take care of me.

Your parents *want* you to learn and accept responsibility. What might they be trying to accomplish in terms of:

Your staying out late? _____

Using the car? _____

Who your friends are? _____

How you spend your money? _____

What you do on dates? _____

How you make decisions? _____

Your staying home alone? _____

The places you go? _____

Your telling the truth? _____

Buying your clothes? _____

Doing your chores? _____

Doing your school work? _____

Ask forgiveness for past irresponsible actions.

Refer back to the question above. List the areas where you have been irresponsible.

_____

_____

It is hard to build trust when actions from the past have not been completely taken care of. The most important step in cleaning up the past is demonstrating to your parents that you realize how wrong you were and that you want them to forgive you.

When asking forgiveness, always include these three

points: 1. I was wrong; 2. I am sorry; 3. Will you forgive me?

Asking forgiveness sometimes isn't enough. You may need to make restitution. Restitution is replacing, repairing or paying for anything you have broken, lost, stolen or misused. What do you need to make restitution for?

_____

_____

Discuss with your parents ways you can be more responsible.

Your parents know you very well. They can help you be more responsible.

So you'll know what to work on first, ask your parents which areas of your irresponsibility bug them the most. To avoid being overwhelmed, ask them to name only three and list them below. Write one step you will take in each area to change your parents' view of you.

1. _____

2. _____

3. _____

Learn the difference between a diligent man and a lazy man.

Read through the Book of Proverbs by reading one chapter a day for one month. Since there are 31 chapters, you may want to read the chapter that corresponds to the day's date. For example, if today is the 6th, read Proverbs 6. If it is the 19th, read Proverbs 19.

As you read, mark a "D" beside the verses that talk about the diligent man and an "L" beside the verses that talk about the lazy, sluggard or slack man. At the end of the month, fill out a chart like the one below.

Diligence:

Verse	What it says	What it means	What I will do
15:19	The path of the diligent is a highway	When one is diligent his life is easier	I must realize that hard work will pay off

Laziness:

Verse	What it says	What it means	What I will do
6:10,11	A little sleep, a little slumber, a little rest will lead to need	If a person is constantly taking it easy he will always be in want of something	I need to do my homework as soon as I get home so I won't make poor grades

If you have trouble following through, ask for help.

For example, if you are supposed to cut the grass and the lawn mower breaks down, instead of just leaving it until your dad gets home, call him and ask what you should do. What is another example?

_____

_____

_____

Keep a list of commitments you make.

Following through on your commitments is a lot easier if you make a list. Beside each commitment write down when it is due and when you will do it. Each day work on the most important commitments first. When you finish a commitment, check it off. Don't let a day pass without fulfilling a commitment you made or working toward accomplishing larger ones.

Here is an example of such a list:

To do	When due	When I will do it
Cut the grass	Saturday	Saturday
Algebra questions	tomorrow	today after school
Write thank you note	next Sunday	tonight after dinner

Develop a servant's heart.

Look for ways to serve your parents . . . even before they ask! When they realize you want what is best for them, and not just what's best for you, they will trust you more.

What are three ways you can serve your parents this week?

1. _____

2. _____

3. _____

Wrapping It Up

To get your parents to trust you more, you must be more responsible. If you want to raise them properly, this is absolutely vital. To put it in a phrase: *Follow through!*

Seek to be as responsible as Jesus by:

1. Making "trust deposits."
2. Seeing responsibility from your parents' perspective.
3. Asking forgiveness for irresponsibility.
4. Talking with your parents about how to be more responsible.
5. Studying the difference between a diligent man and a lazy man and taking action.
6. Asking for help.
7. Keeping a list of commitments.
8. Serving your parents.

Parents' Obedience School
Session #3

1. Check here when you have asked your parents' forgiveness for any irresponsibility on your part. ☐

2. What was the main way your parents said you could be more responsible?

_____

_____

_____

3. For one month keep a record of how well you do in following through on the question above.

4. At the end of one month ask your parents how you're doing. What did they say?

_____

_____

_____

| **Memorize Ephesians 6:1,2** |

My Parents Don't Love Me!

As you read this next scene, try to count the number of errors that this guy makes in raising his parents.

Son: (hurrying up from the table) Oh, I'm late! Great dinner, Mom. I'll be back in a couple of hours. A bunch of us are going to play basketball over at Mike's.

Dad: Is your homework done yet?

Son: (stopping dead still) No, but I didn't have much.

Mom: Don't you have an algebra quiz tomorrow?

Son: Yeah, but it's over an easy chapter.

Dad: (in disbelief) Isn't algebra the class you got a "D" in last semester? How could you even dream of going out tonight? You're not going anywhere.

Son: But they're all counting on me! They won't have even teams without me. We've been planning this all day. I've got to go.

Mom: (sweetly) Don't argue, darling. We know what's best for you.

Son: What's best for me?! You've got to be kidding.

Dad: Don't talk to your mother that way. Get back in your room right now and start studying.

Mom: (trying to ease the situation) We love you, honey.

Son: (shouts) You don't love me! You never have loved me!

Δ   Δ   Δ

If you counted at least seven errors, you're perceptive and have a great chance to train your parents well. If you didn't, go back until you see at least five.

How often have you thought that your parents didn't love you?

☐ Once a year   ☐ Once a day
☐ Once a month   ☐ Once every hour
☐ Once a week   ☐ Other (explain)

Do you really think your parents don't love you? If you think they don't, explain why and give examples.

_____

_____

_____

What do you think "being loved" involves?

_____

_____

What do you think "loving you" means to your parents?

_____

_____

If your parents were brought to trial for not loving you, what would a jury of three parents and three students decide?

☐ Pardon   ☐ Condemn
☐ Split vote

Whether or not you feel loved by your parents has a major impact on the way you feel about yourself.

You can feel . . .
. . . like you're not worth anything.

. . . like nobody will love you if your parents don't.

. . . like you don't measure up.

. . . like you need people's attention constantly.

. . . like you need to succeed in order for them to love you.

. . . angry.

Or you can feel . . .
. . . like you're a valuable, respected, cared for, lovable person.

. . . confident no matter what happens to you.

. . . like it doesn't matter what you do—your parents will always love you.

What are the ways you have felt?

_____

_____

_____

How you feel about yourself has a major effect on how you will succeed in life. How could the above feelings, positive or negative, affect your

Family life? _____

School/Work? _____

Ministry? _____

Friendships? _____

Relationship with God?_____

Many students think their parents don't love them when that's not true at all. Actually their parents love them very much and are trying their best to care for them.

Here is how your thinking may cause you to feel like your parents don't love you:

I want to be, do or have something.

My parents said I can't.

I don't like that.

They know I don't like that.

If they loved me, they would want to please me.

Since they didn't please me, they must not love me.

Have you ever felt like this? Describe the situation.

_____

_____

_____

What were the results?

_____

_____

Jesus was tempted to feel this way, too. Read Hebrews 2:18 for proof.

Return one last time to our story of Jesus in Luke 2:41-51. Read these verses again.

What are the clues Jesus greatly enjoyed what He was doing?

_____

_____

How were Jesus' parents feeling before they found Jesus? Why?

_____

_____

Do you think your parent's love is expressed only when they are calm?

_____

_____

Rephrase verse 48 to sound like your parents.

_____

_____

Does this sound like someone who loves you?

☐ Yes   ☐ No

If you were in Jesus' place, how would you have responded?

_____

_____

How did Jesus respond?

_____

_____

What would enable you to respond like Jesus did? Be practical.

_____

_____

This last question may have stumped you. Below are just a few ideas to help you respond to your parents the way Jesus did.

Recognize the difference between real love and what seems like love.

At times you may think that your parents don't love you, but after you've calmed down you realize that they really do. However, there are some students (although this is very rarely the case) whose parents really don't love them. Before you take any other steps, you must first determine whether your parents love you.

Try to write out the definitions of love from your parents' view and from your view:

Parents: _____

_____

You:_____

_____

After thinking it over, check the appropriate box:

☐ A. I know my parents always love me.

☐ B. At times I feel like my parents don't love me, but I know this is not true.

☐ C. I am not sure.

☐ D. I am convinced my parents do not love me.

If you checked box

A — Continue with the step below.

B — Continue with the step below.

C — Continue with the step below.

D — Begin with the steps on page 57.

Figure out how much you're worth to your parents.

If you ever doubt how very much your parents love you, figure how much money they will spend on you during your first twenty-one years of life.

The following worksheet will help you determine the amount. You may want to ask your parents for any amounts you have a question about.

How Much Are You Worth to Your Parents?[1]

Birth
doctor bills, hospital bills, tests, etc. $4,500
Infancy (first year)
nursery furnishings, feeding equipment,
medical care, food, housing, clothing,
toys, photographs, etc. $5,000
Toddler years (1 to 5 years old)
More food, bigger bed, clothes — bigger
everything — every year! medical and dental care,
kindergarten, more toys, etc. $30,000
Childhood (6 to 12 years old)
A lot more food, furniture, medical and dental
care, music lessons, sports equipment, etc. $48,000
Teenager (13 to 17 years old)
Still *more* food, plus fast food, new
furniture, braces, more camps, stereo, etc. $45,000
College Student (18 to 21 years old)
Tuition, room and board, books and supplies,
transportation, clothes, and . . . food! $72,000

GRAND TOTAL   **$204,500**

How much are you worth to your parents? All this money *and a whole lot more!* Their provision is only one indication of how much they love you, but it's a good one.

See how much your parents serve you.

Money isn't the only proof your parents love you. Serving someone is an even greater evidence of love.

What are the ways your parents serve you?

1. _____

2. _____

3. _____

4. _____

5. _____

Think about this: How many plates, glasses, forks, knives, spoons, pots and pans does your mom wash for you each day? Multiply that by 365. What does that total each year? _____ And don't forget all the tasks your dad did to the car or around the house to make life more comfortable for you and your family. Think of the number of days your parents work to provide for you. How many of those mornings do you think they would rather stay home and relax? _____

See how much your parents sacrifice for you.

You may argue that your mom and dad have to cook meals or wash clothes anyway—it can't be that much trouble to wash a few more plates or fold a few more clothes. That may be true, but consider how much they sacrifice for you.

Who stays up all night with you when you are sick? Who works extra hours to pay for all the things you want?

What are some other ways they sacrifice for you?

1. _____

2. _____

3. _____

4. _____

5. _____

Learn to translate what your parents say.

Parents have a funny way of talking sometimes.

They say, "Five A's and one B. Why didn't you make straight A's?"

Instead of, "All A's and one B! That's great!"

They say, "Where have you been?! It's one o'clock in the morning!"

Instead of, "Are you all right? I was concerned about you."

Let's find out what makes them respond like they do. Take the story of Jesus:

1. His parents discover He is missing, so they start looking for Him. Why? They love Him.

2. They can't find Him, so they get anxious and upset. Why? They love Him.

3. They find Him, but instead of rejoicing, they scold Him. Why? They love Him.

Doesn't make sense, does it?

If they hadn't been worried and upset, they would have rejoiced. But all they were thinking was, *Jesus, don't do that again; we don't want you exposed to any harm.*

Make any sense now?

For practice, translate what the parents are really saying in the opening scene of this chapter.

Be understanding with your parents.

Parents are under pressure, too! This pressure may cause them to act like they don't love you.

What pressures are your parents under . . .

In their marriage? _____

Financially? _____

At work? _____

With their own parents? _____

Other? _____

Be patient with your parents.

Your parents are human (whether you believe it or not). They have weaknesses, too. Be patient with them. Allow God to continue working on them.

In what ways have you been impatient with your parents?

_____

_____

How can you be more patient with them? (For starters, read Galatians 5:22,23.)

_____

_____

Pray regularly for your parents.

When you see the pressures and needs of your parents, you can help them by praying for them.

When will you pray each day for your parents?

_____

_____

What can you pray for them?

_____

_____

Love your parents regardless
of their love for you.

Read John 13:34,35. Below are ways you can express love to your parents. Add five additional ways to this list.

1. Say "I love you."

2. Invite your parents to school activities.

3. Visit Dad at his office.

4. Bring Mom flowers.

5. Wash the car without being asked.

6. _____

7. _____

8. _____

9. _____

10. _____

If your parents really don't love you . . .

The next two steps will help you if you know your parents really don't love you. But even if you're convinced your parents love you, there *will* be times when you *feel* like they don't. In either case, you need to be convinced of God's love for you and take security in His love first.

Find peace in God's love.

Only God can ultimately meet your needs. He loves you and thinks you're the greatest.

What do these Scriptures tell you about God's love for you?

Romans 5:8 _____

_____

Ephesians 2:4-7 _____

_____

Ephesians 3:14-19 _____

_____

When your parents reject you, realize that they may have problems and struggles of their own. Possibly they weren't loved themselves when they were children. When they hurt you, take a two-step response:

Step #1—Fall back on God's love. Let Him soothe your pain. Talk it over with Him in private, where you can pound your fists, yell and cry.

Step #2—Bounce back to love your parents. What your folks need most, like anyone else, is love. You may be the only source where they can find it. It is always hard to love those who hurt you, but experiencing God's love will enable you to do this.

Talk it over with someone.

It always helps to get guidance from someone wiser. Your youth minister or Sunday school teacher is a good place to start.

Who will you confide in? _____

Wrapping It Up

Many students feel like their parents don't love them. Very seldom, though, is this the case. Most of the time it is just the way they feel in a particular situation.

You need to learn to respond like Jesus did when you feel this way. Understand that your parents really do love you and are trying to care for you. In a phrase: *Press on!*

To confirm that they love you —
   1. Recognize the difference between real love and what seems like real love.
   2. Figure out how much you're worth to them.
   3. See how much they serve you.
   4. See how much they sacrifice for you.

To respond better when you feel like they don't love you —
   5. Learn to translate.
   6. Understand them.
   7. Be patient with them.
   8. Pray for them.
   9. Express gratefulness.
   10. Love them regardless.

If they really don't love you —
   11. Find peace in God's love.
   12. Talk to someone about it.

When you put these steps into practice, you will find your parents turning out well after all.

Parents' Obedience School
Session #4

1. What three expressions of love mean the most to your parents?

   (1) _____

   (2) _____

   (3) _____

2. Write down a conversation you had with your parents this week and translate it.

_____

_____

_____

3. What two pressures are your parents under right now? (If you're not sure, ask them.)

    (1) _____

    (2) _____

4. Write down a prayer for your parents concerning their struggles and loves. Ask God to answer your prayer.

_____

_____

_____

5. What irritates you the most about your parents? How will you respond next time they do this?

_____

_____

_____

Memorize Matthew 7:12

---

1. Adapted from *The Trouble With Parents* by Tim Stafford (Grand Rapids, MI: Zondervan Publishing House, 1978), pp. 43-45

A Few Last Words

Raising parents in today's society is a hard job. Whenever you see your parents "misbehaving," remember to look at yourself first! For your parents to change, you must change. As you take your focus off of your parents and put it on yourself, you will soon discover that your family is undergoing a wonderful transformation.

May God give you the patience and teachable attitude to raise perfect parents!